LIFE SCRIPTED

Crafting Your Future

CAROLINE TOWERS

LIFE SCRIPTED

Copyright © 2024 CST Creative Limited

ISBN:978-1-7391000-3-2

CAROLINE TOWERS
CAROLINETOWERS.CO.UK

EVERY WORD YOU WRITE IS A STEP TOWARDS
THE LIFE YOU ASPIRE TO CREATE.

"I took my power in my hand and went against the world."

- Emily Dickinson

Welcome to Life Scripted

This journal is your companion in scripting the life you've always imagined. It's more than just a place to write; it's a tool to help you manifest your dreams, set your intentions, and celebrate your achievements.

How to Use This Journal:

Decide your Day: Start each day by writing down how you want your day to go, what you want to achieve or how you want to feel. This sets a positive tone and gives direction to your day.

Gratitude Practice: at the end of the day write down what you're thankful for. Gratitude turns what we have into enough, and more.

Reflect and Revise: Look back on the day and reflect on what went well and revise any moments you would have liked to have gone differently.

Remember, there are no rules. This journal is your safe space to dream, plan, and grow. Every word you write brings you a step closer to the life you're scripting for yourself.

Your journey is uniquely yours. Let the pages of 'Life Scripted' be the canvas of your life.

Happy scripting!

Caroline XOXO

DATE: _____

TODAY WILL BE:

TODAY I AM GRATEFUL FOR:

TODAY I REFLECT ON:

DATE: _____

TODAY WILL BE:

TODAY I AM GRATEFUL FOR:

TODAY I REFLECT ON:

DATE: _____

TODAY WILL BE:

_____
_____
_____
_____
_____
_____
_____
_____
_____
_____
_____
_____
_____
_____
_____
_____
_____
_____
_____
_____
_____
_____
_____
_____
_____
_____
_____
_____

TODAY I AM GRATEFUL FOR:

TODAY I REFLECT ON:

DATE: _____

TODAY WILL BE:

_____
_____
_____
_____
_____
_____
_____
_____
_____
_____
_____
_____
_____
_____
_____
_____
_____
_____
_____
_____
_____
_____
_____
_____
_____
_____
_____

TODAY I AM GRATEFUL FOR:

TODAY I REFLECT ON:

DATE: _____

TODAY WILL BE:

_____
_____
_____
_____
_____
_____
_____
_____
_____
_____
_____
_____
_____
_____
_____
_____
_____
_____
_____
_____
_____
_____
_____
_____
_____
_____
_____
_____
_____

TODAY I AM GRATEFUL FOR:

TODAY I REFLECT ON:

DATE: _____

TODAY WILL BE:

_____
_____
_____
_____
_____
_____
_____
_____
_____
_____
_____
_____
_____
_____
_____
_____
_____
_____
_____
_____
_____
_____
_____
_____
_____
_____

TODAY I AM GRATEFUL FOR:

TODAY I REFLECT ON:

DATE: _____

TODAY WILL BE:

_____
_____
_____
_____
_____
_____
_____
_____
_____
_____
_____
_____
_____
_____
_____
_____
_____
_____
_____
_____
_____
_____
_____
_____
_____
_____
_____
_____

TODAY I AM GRATEFUL FOR:

TODAY I REFLECT ON:

DATE:_____

TODAY WILL BE:

TODAY I AM GRATEFUL FOR:

TODAY I REFLECT ON:

DATE:_____

TODAY WILL BE:

TODAY I AM GRATEFUL FOR:

TODAY I REFLECT ON:

DATE: _____

TODAY WILL BE:

_____
_____
_____
_____
_____
_____
_____
_____
_____
_____
_____
_____
_____
_____
_____
_____
_____
_____
_____
_____
_____
_____
_____
_____
_____
_____
_____
_____

TODAY I AM GRATEFUL FOR:

TODAY I REFLECT ON:

DATE: _____

TODAY WILL BE:

_____
_____
_____
_____
_____
_____
_____
_____
_____
_____
_____
_____
_____
_____
_____
_____
_____
_____
_____
_____
_____
_____
_____
_____
_____
_____
_____

TODAY I AM GRATEFUL FOR:

TODAY I REFLECT ON:

DATE: _____

TODAY WILL BE:

TODAY I AM GRATEFUL FOR:

TODAY I REFLECT ON:

DATE: _____

TODAY WILL BE:

TODAY I AM GRATEFUL FOR:

TODAY I REFLECT ON:

DATE: _____

TODAY WILL BE:

_____
_____
_____
_____
_____
_____
_____
_____
_____
_____
_____
_____
_____
_____
_____
_____
_____
_____
_____
_____
_____
_____
_____
_____
_____
_____
_____
_____

TODAY I AM GRATEFUL FOR:

TODAY I REFLECT ON:

DATE: _____

TODAY WILL BE:

_____
_____
_____
_____
_____
_____
_____
_____
_____
_____
_____
_____
_____
_____
_____
_____
_____
_____
_____
_____
_____
_____
_____
_____
_____
_____
_____

TODAY I AM GRATEFUL FOR:

TODAY I REFLECT ON:

DATE: _____

TODAY WILL BE:

_____
_____
_____
_____
_____
_____
_____
_____
_____
_____
_____
_____
_____
_____
_____
_____
_____
_____
_____
_____
_____
_____
_____
_____
_____
_____
_____
_____

TODAY I AM GRATEFUL FOR:

TODAY I REFLECT ON:

DATE:

TODAY WILL BE:

_____
_____
_____
_____
_____
_____
_____
_____
_____
_____
_____
_____
_____
_____
_____
_____
_____
_____
_____
_____
_____
_____
_____
_____
_____
_____

TODAY I AM GRATEFUL FOR:

TODAY I REFLECT ON:

DATE: _____

TODAY WILL BE:

_____
_____
_____
_____
_____
_____
_____
_____
_____
_____
_____
_____
_____
_____
_____
_____
_____
_____
_____
_____
_____
_____
_____
_____
_____
_____
_____
_____

TODAY I AM GRATEFUL FOR:

TODAY I REFLECT ON:

DATE: _____

TODAY WILL BE:

_____
_____
_____
_____
_____
_____
_____
_____
_____
_____
_____
_____
_____
_____
_____
_____
_____
_____
_____
_____
_____
_____
_____
_____
_____
_____
_____
_____
_____
_____
_____

TODAY I AM GRATEFUL FOR:

TODAY I REFLECT ON:

DATE: _____

TODAY WILL BE:

_____
_____
_____
_____
_____
_____
_____
_____
_____
_____
_____
_____
_____
_____
_____
_____
_____
_____
_____
_____
_____
_____
_____
_____
_____
_____
_____
_____
_____

TODAY I AM GRATEFUL FOR:

TODAY I REFLECT ON:

DATE: _____

TODAY WILL BE:

_____
_____
_____
_____
_____
_____
_____
_____
_____
_____
_____
_____
_____
_____
_____
_____
_____
_____
_____
_____
_____
_____
_____
_____
_____
_____
_____
_____
_____

TODAY I AM GRATEFUL FOR:

TODAY I REFLECT ON:

DATE: _____

TODAY WILL BE:

TODAY I AM GRATEFUL FOR:

TODAY I REFLECT ON:

DATE: _____

TODAY WILL BE:

_____
_____
_____
_____
_____
_____
_____
_____
_____
_____
_____
_____
_____
_____
_____
_____
_____
_____
_____
_____
_____
_____
_____
_____
_____
_____
_____
_____

TODAY I AM GRATEFUL FOR:

TODAY I REFLECT ON:

DATE:_____

TODAY WILL BE:

TODAY I AM GRATEFUL FOR:

TODAY I REFLECT ON:

DATE: _____

TODAY WILL BE:

TODAY I AM GRATEFUL FOR:

TODAY I REFLECT ON:

DATE: _____

TODAY WILL BE:

_____
_____
_____
_____
_____
_____
_____
_____
_____
_____
_____
_____
_____
_____
_____
_____
_____
_____
_____
_____
_____
_____
_____
_____
_____
_____
_____
_____
_____
_____
_____

TODAY I AM GRATEFUL FOR:

TODAY I REFLECT ON:

DATE:_____

TODAY WILL BE:

TODAY I AM GRATEFUL FOR:

TODAY I REFLECT ON:

DATE: _____

TODAY WILL BE:

TODAY I AM GRATEFUL FOR:

TODAY I REFLECT ON:

DATE: _____

TODAY WILL BE:

_____
_____
_____
_____
_____
_____
_____
_____
_____
_____
_____
_____
_____
_____
_____
_____
_____
_____
_____
_____
_____
_____
_____
_____
_____

TODAY I AM GRATEFUL FOR:

TODAY I REFLECT ON:

DATE: _____

TODAY WILL BE:

_____
_____
_____
_____
_____
_____
_____
_____
_____
_____
_____
_____
_____
_____
_____
_____
_____
_____
_____
_____
_____
_____
_____
_____
_____
_____
_____
_____

TODAY I AM GRATEFUL FOR:

TODAY I REFLECT ON:

DATE: _____

TODAY WILL BE:

TODAY I AM GRATEFUL FOR:

TODAY I REFLECT ON:

DATE: _____

TODAY WILL BE:

_____
_____
_____
_____
_____
_____
_____
_____
_____
_____
_____
_____
_____
_____
_____
_____
_____
_____
_____
_____
_____
_____
_____
_____
_____

TODAY I AM GRATEFUL FOR:

TODAY I REFLECT ON:

DATE:＿＿＿＿＿＿＿＿＿＿＿＿

TODAY WILL BE:

_____
_____
_____
_____
_____
_____
_____
_____
_____
_____
_____
_____
_____
_____
_____
_____
_____
_____
_____
_____
_____
_____
_____
_____
_____
_____
_____
_____

TODAY I AM GRATEFUL FOR:

TODAY I REFLECT ON:

DATE: _____

TODAY WILL BE:

_____
_____
_____
_____
_____
_____
_____
_____
_____
_____
_____
_____
_____
_____
_____
_____
_____
_____
_____
_____
_____
_____
_____
_____
_____
_____
_____
_____
_____
_____

TODAY I AM GRATEFUL FOR:

TODAY I REFLECT ON:

DATE: _____

TODAY WILL BE:

TODAY I AM GRATEFUL FOR:

TODAY I REFLECT ON:

DATE: _____

TODAY WILL BE:

_____
_____
_____
_____
_____
_____
_____
_____
_____
_____
_____
_____
_____
_____
_____
_____
_____
_____
_____
_____
_____
_____
_____
_____
_____
_____
_____
_____
_____
_____
_____

TODAY I AM GRATEFUL FOR:

TODAY I REFLECT ON:

DATE: _____

TODAY WILL BE:

TODAY I AM GRATEFUL FOR:

TODAY I REFLECT ON:

DATE: _____

TODAY WILL BE:

_____
_____
_____
_____
_____
_____
_____
_____
_____
_____
_____
_____
_____
_____
_____
_____
_____
_____
_____
_____
_____
_____
_____
_____
_____
_____
_____
_____

TODAY I AM GRATEFUL FOR:

TODAY I REFLECT ON:

DATE: _____

TODAY WILL BE:

_____
_____
_____
_____
_____
_____
_____
_____
_____
_____
_____
_____
_____
_____
_____
_____
_____
_____
_____
_____
_____
_____
_____
_____
_____
_____

TODAY I AM GRATEFUL FOR:

TODAY I REFLECT ON:

DATE: _____

TODAY WILL BE:

_____
_____
_____
_____
_____
_____
_____
_____
_____
_____
_____
_____
_____
_____
_____
_____
_____
_____
_____
_____
_____
_____
_____
_____
_____
_____
_____
_____

TODAY I AM GRATEFUL FOR:

TODAY I REFLECT ON:

DATE: _____

TODAY WILL BE:

_____
_____
_____
_____
_____
_____
_____
_____
_____
_____
_____
_____
_____
_____
_____
_____
_____
_____
_____
_____
_____
_____
_____
_____
_____
_____
_____
_____

TODAY I AM GRATEFUL FOR:

TODAY I REFLECT ON:

DATE: _____

TODAY WILL BE:

TODAY I AM GRATEFUL FOR:

TODAY I REFLECT ON:

DATE: _____

TODAY WILL BE:

TODAY I AM GRATEFUL FOR:

TODAY I REFLECT ON:

DATE: _____

TODAY WILL BE:

TODAY I AM GRATEFUL FOR:

TODAY I REFLECT ON:

DATE: _____

TODAY WILL BE:

TODAY I AM GRATEFUL FOR:

TODAY I REFLECT ON:

DATE: _____

TODAY WILL BE:

_____
_____
_____
_____
_____
_____
_____
_____
_____
_____
_____
_____
_____
_____
_____
_____
_____
_____
_____
_____
_____
_____
_____
_____
_____
_____
_____
_____
_____

TODAY I AM GRATEFUL FOR:

TODAY I REFLECT ON:

DATE: _____

TODAY WILL BE:

_____

_____

_____

_____

_____

_____

_____

_____

_____

_____

_____

_____

_____

_____

_____

_____

_____

_____

_____

_____

_____

_____

_____

_____

_____

_____

TODAY I AM GRATEFUL FOR:

TODAY I REFLECT ON:

DATE: _____

TODAY WILL BE:

_____
_____
_____
_____
_____
_____
_____
_____
_____
_____
_____
_____
_____
_____
_____
_____
_____
_____
_____
_____
_____
_____
_____
_____
_____
_____

TODAY I AM GRATEFUL FOR:

TODAY I REFLECT ON:

DATE:_____

TODAY WILL BE:

_____
_____
_____
_____
_____
_____
_____
_____
_____
_____
_____
_____
_____
_____
_____
_____
_____
_____
_____
_____
_____
_____
_____
_____
_____
_____
_____
_____

TODAY I AM GRATEFUL FOR:

TODAY I REFLECT ON:

DATE: _____

TODAY WILL BE:

_____
_____
_____
_____
_____
_____
_____
_____
_____
_____
_____
_____
_____
_____
_____
_____
_____
_____
_____
_____
_____
_____
_____
_____
_____
_____
_____
_____

TODAY I AM GRATEFUL FOR:

TODAY I REFLECT ON:

DATE: _____

TODAY WILL BE:

_____
_____
_____
_____
_____
_____
_____
_____
_____
_____
_____
_____
_____
_____
_____
_____
_____
_____
_____
_____
_____
_____
_____
_____
_____
_____
_____
_____
_____
_____

TODAY I AM GRATEFUL FOR:

TODAY I REFLECT ON:

DATE: _____

TODAY WILL BE:

_____
_____
_____
_____
_____
_____
_____
_____
_____
_____
_____
_____
_____
_____
_____
_____
_____
_____
_____
_____
_____
_____
_____
_____
_____
_____
_____

TODAY I AM GRATEFUL FOR:

TODAY I REFLECT ON:

DATE: _____

TODAY WILL BE:

TODAY I AM GRATEFUL FOR:

TODAY I REFLECT ON:

DATE: _____

TODAY WILL BE:

_____
_____
_____
_____
_____
_____
_____
_____
_____
_____
_____
_____
_____
_____
_____
_____
_____
_____
_____
_____
_____
_____
_____
_____
_____
_____
_____
_____
_____
_____

TODAY I AM GRATEFUL FOR:

TODAY I REFLECT ON:

DATE:_____

TODAY WILL BE:

_____
_____
_____
_____
_____
_____
_____
_____
_____
_____
_____
_____
_____
_____
_____
_____
_____
_____
_____
_____
_____
_____
_____
_____
_____
_____
_____
_____

TODAY I AM GRATEFUL FOR:

TODAY I REFLECT ON:

DATE: _____

TODAY WILL BE:

_____
_____
_____
_____
_____
_____
_____
_____
_____
_____
_____
_____
_____
_____
_____
_____
_____
_____
_____
_____
_____
_____
_____
_____
_____
_____

TODAY I AM GRATEFUL FOR:

TODAY I REFLECT ON:

DATE: _____

TODAY WILL BE:

_____
_____
_____
_____
_____
_____
_____
_____
_____
_____
_____
_____
_____
_____
_____
_____
_____
_____
_____
_____
_____
_____
_____
_____
_____
_____
_____
_____
_____
_____

TODAY I AM GRATEFUL FOR:

TODAY I REFLECT ON:

DATE: _____

TODAY WILL BE:

_____
_____
_____
_____
_____
_____
_____
_____
_____
_____
_____
_____
_____
_____
_____
_____
_____
_____
_____
_____
_____
_____
_____
_____
_____
_____
_____
_____

TODAY I AM GRATEFUL FOR:

TODAY I REFLECT ON:

DATE: _____

TODAY WILL BE:

_____
_____
_____
_____
_____
_____
_____
_____
_____
_____
_____
_____
_____
_____
_____
_____
_____
_____
_____
_____
_____
_____
_____
_____
_____
_____
_____
_____
_____

TODAY I AM GRATEFUL FOR:

TODAY I REFLECT ON:

DATE: _____

TODAY WILL BE:

_____
_____
_____
_____
_____
_____
_____
_____
_____
_____
_____
_____
_____
_____
_____
_____
_____
_____
_____
_____
_____
_____
_____
_____
_____
_____
_____

TODAY I AM GRATEFUL FOR:

TODAY I REFLECT ON:

DATE:_____

TODAY WILL BE:

TODAY I AM GRATEFUL FOR:

TODAY I REFLECT ON:

DATE: _____

TODAY WILL BE:

_____
_____
_____
_____
_____
_____
_____
_____
_____
_____
_____
_____
_____
_____
_____
_____
_____
_____
_____
_____
_____
_____
_____
_____
_____
_____
_____
_____

TODAY I AM GRATEFUL FOR:

TODAY I REFLECT ON:

DATE: _____

TODAY WILL BE:

_____
_____
_____
_____
_____
_____
_____
_____
_____
_____
_____
_____
_____
_____
_____
_____
_____
_____
_____
_____
_____
_____
_____
_____
_____
_____
_____
_____
_____

TODAY I AM GRATEFUL FOR:

TODAY I REFLECT ON:

DATE:_____

TODAY WILL BE:

_____
_____
_____
_____
_____
_____
_____
_____
_____
_____
_____
_____
_____
_____
_____
_____
_____
_____
_____
_____
_____
_____
_____
_____
_____
_____
_____
_____

TODAY I AM GRATEFUL FOR:

TODAY I REFLECT ON:

DATE:_____

TODAY WILL BE:

_____
_____
_____
_____
_____
_____
_____
_____
_____
_____
_____
_____
_____
_____
_____
_____
_____
_____
_____
_____
_____
_____
_____
_____
_____
_____

TODAY I AM GRATEFUL FOR:

TODAY I REFLECT ON:

DATE: _____

TODAY WILL BE:

_____
_____
_____
_____
_____
_____
_____
_____
_____
_____
_____
_____
_____
_____
_____
_____
_____
_____
_____
_____
_____
_____
_____
_____
_____
_____
_____

TODAY I AM GRATEFUL FOR:

TODAY I REFLECT ON:

DATE: _____

TODAY WILL BE:

TODAY I AM GRATEFUL FOR:

TODAY I REFLECT ON:

DATE:_____

TODAY WILL BE:

TODAY I AM GRATEFUL FOR:

TODAY I REFLECT ON:

DATE: _____

TODAY WILL BE:

TODAY I AM GRATEFUL FOR:

TODAY I REFLECT ON:

DATE: _____

TODAY WILL BE:

_____
_____
_____
_____
_____
_____
_____
_____
_____
_____
_____
_____
_____
_____
_____
_____
_____
_____
_____
_____
_____
_____
_____
_____
_____
_____
_____

TODAY I AM GRATEFUL FOR:

TODAY I REFLECT ON:

DATE: _____

TODAY WILL BE:

_____
_____
_____
_____
_____
_____
_____
_____
_____
_____
_____
_____
_____
_____
_____
_____
_____
_____
_____
_____
_____
_____
_____
_____
_____
_____
_____
_____

TODAY I AM GRATEFUL FOR:

TODAY I REFLECT ON:

DATE: _____

TODAY WILL BE:

_____
_____
_____
_____
_____
_____
_____
_____
_____
_____
_____
_____
_____
_____
_____
_____
_____
_____
_____
_____
_____
_____
_____
_____
_____
_____
_____
_____

TODAY I AM GRATEFUL FOR:

TODAY I REFLECT ON:

DATE: _____

TODAY WILL BE:

_____
_____
_____
_____
_____
_____
_____
_____
_____
_____
_____
_____
_____
_____
_____
_____
_____
_____
_____
_____
_____
_____
_____
_____
_____
_____
_____
_____

TODAY I AM GRATEFUL FOR:

TODAY I REFLECT ON:

DATE: _____

TODAY WILL BE:

TODAY I AM GRATEFUL FOR:

TODAY I REFLECT ON:

DATE: _____

TODAY WILL BE:

TODAY I AM GRATEFUL FOR:

TODAY I REFLECT ON:

DATE: _____

TODAY WILL BE:

_____
_____
_____
_____
_____
_____
_____
_____
_____
_____
_____
_____
_____
_____
_____
_____
_____
_____
_____
_____
_____
_____
_____
_____
_____

TODAY I AM GRATEFUL FOR:

TODAY I REFLECT ON:

DATE: _____

TODAY WILL BE:

_____
_____
_____
_____
_____
_____
_____
_____
_____
_____
_____
_____
_____
_____
_____
_____
_____
_____
_____
_____
_____
_____
_____
_____
_____
_____

TODAY I AM GRATEFUL FOR:

TODAY I REFLECT ON:

DATE: _____

TODAY WILL BE:

TODAY I AM GRATEFUL FOR:

TODAY I REFLECT ON:

DATE:_____

TODAY WILL BE:

TODAY I AM GRATEFUL FOR:

TODAY I REFLECT ON:

DATE: _____

TODAY WILL BE:

_____
_____
_____
_____
_____
_____
_____
_____
_____
_____
_____
_____
_____
_____
_____
_____
_____
_____
_____
_____
_____
_____
_____
_____
_____
_____
_____
_____
_____

TODAY I AM GRATEFUL FOR:

TODAY I REFLECT ON:

DATE: _____

TODAY WILL BE:

_____
_____
_____
_____
_____
_____
_____
_____
_____
_____
_____
_____
_____
_____
_____
_____
_____
_____
_____
_____
_____
_____
_____
_____
_____
_____
_____

TODAY I AM GRATEFUL FOR:

TODAY I REFLECT ON:

DATE: _____

TODAY WILL BE:

_____
_____
_____
_____
_____
_____
_____
_____
_____
_____
_____
_____
_____
_____
_____
_____
_____
_____
_____
_____
_____
_____
_____
_____
_____
_____
_____
_____
_____

TODAY I AM GRATEFUL FOR:

TODAY I REFLECT ON:

DATE: _____

TODAY WILL BE:

_____

_____

_____

_____

_____

_____

_____

_____

_____

_____

_____

_____

_____

_____

_____

_____

_____

_____

_____

_____

_____

_____

_____

_____

_____

_____

_____

_____

TODAY I AM GRATEFUL FOR:

TODAY I REFLECT ON:

DATE:_____

TODAY WILL BE:

TODAY I AM GRATEFUL FOR:

TODAY I REFLECT ON:

DATE: _____

TODAY WILL BE:

TODAY I AM GRATEFUL FOR:

TODAY I REFLECT ON:

DATE:_____

TODAY WILL BE:

_____
_____
_____
_____
_____
_____
_____
_____
_____
_____
_____
_____
_____
_____
_____
_____
_____
_____
_____
_____
_____
_____
_____
_____
_____
_____

TODAY I AM GRATEFUL FOR:

TODAY I REFLECT ON:

DATE: _____

TODAY WILL BE:

TODAY I AM GRATEFUL FOR:

TODAY I REFLECT ON:

DATE: _____

TODAY WILL BE:

_____
_____
_____
_____
_____
_____
_____
_____
_____
_____
_____
_____
_____
_____
_____
_____
_____
_____
_____
_____
_____
_____
_____
_____
_____
_____
_____

TODAY I AM GRATEFUL FOR:

TODAY I REFLECT ON:

DATE:_____

TODAY WILL BE:

TODAY I AM GRATEFUL FOR:

TODAY I REFLECT ON:

DATE: _____

TODAY WILL BE:

_____
_____
_____
_____
_____
_____
_____
_____
_____
_____
_____
_____
_____
_____
_____
_____
_____
_____
_____
_____
_____
_____
_____
_____
_____
_____

TODAY I AM GRATEFUL FOR:

TODAY I REFLECT ON:

DATE: _____

TODAY WILL BE:

_____
_____
_____
_____
_____
_____
_____
_____
_____
_____
_____
_____
_____
_____
_____
_____
_____
_____
_____
_____
_____
_____
_____
_____
_____
_____
_____
_____

TODAY I AM GRATEFUL FOR:

TODAY I REFLECT ON:

DATE:_____

TODAY WILL BE:

TODAY I AM GRATEFUL FOR:

TODAY I REFLECT ON:

DATE:

TODAY WILL BE:

TODAY I AM GRATEFUL FOR:

TODAY I REFLECT ON:

DATE: _____

TODAY WILL BE:

_____
_____
_____
_____
_____
_____
_____
_____
_____
_____
_____
_____
_____
_____
_____
_____
_____
_____
_____
_____
_____
_____
_____
_____
_____
_____
_____
_____
_____

TODAY I AM GRATEFUL FOR:

TODAY I REFLECT ON:

DATE: _____

TODAY WILL BE:

_____
_____
_____
_____
_____
_____
_____
_____
_____
_____
_____
_____
_____
_____
_____
_____
_____
_____
_____
_____
_____
_____
_____
_____
_____
_____
_____
_____
_____

TODAY I AM GRATEFUL FOR:

TODAY I REFLECT ON:

DATE: _____

TODAY WILL BE:

_____
_____
_____
_____
_____
_____
_____
_____
_____
_____
_____
_____
_____
_____
_____
_____
_____
_____
_____
_____
_____
_____
_____
_____
_____
_____
_____

TODAY I AM GRATEFUL FOR:

TODAY I REFLECT ON:

DATE: _____

TODAY WILL BE:

_____
_____
_____
_____
_____
_____
_____
_____
_____
_____
_____
_____
_____
_____
_____
_____
_____
_____
_____
_____
_____
_____
_____
_____
_____

TODAY I AM GRATEFUL FOR:

TODAY I REFLECT ON:

DATE:_____

TODAY WILL BE:

TODAY I AM GRATEFUL FOR:

TODAY I REFLECT ON:

DATE: _____

TODAY WILL BE:

TODAY I AM GRATEFUL FOR:

TODAY I REFLECT ON:

DATE:_____

TODAY WILL BE:

_____
_____
_____
_____
_____
_____
_____
_____
_____
_____
_____
_____
_____
_____
_____
_____
_____
_____
_____
_____
_____
_____
_____
_____
_____
_____
_____
_____

TODAY I AM GRATEFUL FOR:

TODAY I REFLECT ON:

DATE: _____

TODAY WILL BE:

_____
_____
_____
_____
_____
_____
_____
_____
_____
_____
_____
_____
_____
_____
_____
_____
_____
_____
_____
_____
_____
_____
_____
_____
_____

TODAY I AM GRATEFUL FOR:

TODAY I REFLECT ON:

DATE: _____

TODAY WILL BE:

_____

_____

_____

_____

_____

_____

_____

_____

_____

_____

_____

_____

_____

_____

_____

_____

_____

_____

_____

_____

_____

_____

_____

_____

_____

TODAY I AM GRATEFUL FOR:

TODAY I REFLECT ON:

DATE: _____

TODAY WILL BE:

_____
_____
_____
_____
_____
_____
_____
_____
_____
_____
_____
_____
_____
_____
_____
_____
_____
_____
_____
_____
_____
_____
_____
_____
_____
_____
_____
_____

TODAY I AM GRATEFUL FOR:

TODAY I REFLECT ON:

DATE: _____

TODAY WILL BE:

_____
_____
_____
_____
_____
_____
_____
_____
_____
_____
_____
_____
_____
_____
_____
_____
_____
_____
_____
_____
_____
_____
_____
_____
_____
_____

TODAY I AM GRATEFUL FOR:

TODAY I REFLECT ON:

DATE: _____

TODAY WILL BE:

TODAY I AM GRATEFUL FOR:

TODAY I REFLECT ON:

DATE:_____

TODAY WILL BE:

TODAY I AM GRATEFUL FOR:

TODAY I REFLECT ON:

DATE:_____

TODAY WILL BE:

TODAY I AM GRATEFUL FOR:

TODAY I REFLECT ON:

DATE:_____

TODAY WILL BE:

TODAY I AM GRATEFUL FOR:

TODAY I REFLECT ON:

DATE: _____

TODAY WILL BE:

TODAY I AM GRATEFUL FOR:

TODAY I REFLECT ON:

DATE: _____

TODAY WILL BE:

_____
_____
_____
_____
_____
_____
_____
_____
_____
_____
_____
_____
_____
_____
_____
_____
_____
_____
_____
_____
_____
_____
_____
_____
_____
_____
_____
_____
_____

TODAY I AM GRATEFUL FOR:

TODAY I REFLECT ON:

DATE: _____

TODAY WILL BE:

_____
_____
_____
_____
_____
_____
_____
_____
_____
_____
_____
_____
_____
_____
_____
_____
_____
_____
_____
_____
_____
_____
_____
_____
_____
_____
_____
_____

TODAY I AM GRATEFUL FOR:

TODAY I REFLECT ON:

DATE: _____

TODAY WILL BE:

_____
_____
_____
_____
_____
_____
_____
_____
_____
_____
_____
_____
_____
_____
_____
_____
_____
_____
_____
_____
_____
_____
_____
_____
_____
_____
_____
_____
_____

TODAY I AM GRATEFUL FOR:

TODAY I REFLECT ON:

DATE: _____

TODAY WILL BE:

TODAY I AM GRATEFUL FOR:

TODAY I REFLECT ON:

DATE: _____

TODAY WILL BE:

TODAY I AM GRATEFUL FOR:

TODAY I REFLECT ON:

DATE: _____

TODAY WILL BE:

_____
_____
_____
_____
_____
_____
_____
_____
_____
_____
_____
_____
_____
_____
_____
_____
_____
_____
_____
_____
_____
_____
_____
_____
_____
_____

TODAY I AM GRATEFUL FOR:

TODAY I REFLECT ON:

DATE: _____

TODAY WILL BE:

_____
_____
_____
_____
_____
_____
_____
_____
_____
_____
_____
_____
_____
_____
_____
_____
_____
_____
_____
_____
_____
_____
_____
_____
_____

TODAY I AM GRATEFUL FOR:

TODAY I REFLECT ON:

DATE: _____

TODAY WILL BE:

TODAY I AM GRATEFUL FOR:

TODAY I REFLECT ON:

DATE: _____

TODAY WILL BE:

_____
_____
_____
_____
_____
_____
_____
_____
_____
_____
_____
_____
_____
_____
_____
_____
_____
_____
_____
_____
_____
_____
_____
_____
_____
_____
_____
_____
_____
_____

TODAY I AM GRATEFUL FOR:

TODAY I REFLECT ON:

DATE: _____

TODAY WILL BE:

TODAY I AM GRATEFUL FOR:

TODAY I REFLECT ON:

DATE: _____

TODAY WILL BE:

TODAY I AM GRATEFUL FOR:

TODAY I REFLECT ON:

DATE: _____

TODAY WILL BE:

_____
_____
_____
_____
_____
_____
_____
_____
_____
_____
_____
_____
_____
_____
_____
_____
_____
_____
_____
_____
_____
_____
_____
_____
_____
_____
_____
_____

TODAY I AM GRATEFUL FOR:

TODAY I REFLECT ON: